CATCH THE THIEVES WITH YOUR HIDDEN RICHES

by Robert E. Bolden

**Vision
Publishing**

The Lord gave the word: great was the company of those that published it.
— **Psalm 68:11**

Catch the Thieves With Your Hidden Riches
ISBN 0-9651783-1-5
Copyright © 2001 by
Robert E. Bolden
Published by Vision Publishing
P.O. Box 11166
Carson, California 90746-1166

Published by:
Vision Publishing
P.O. Box 11166
Carson, California 90746

DEDICATION

This book is dedicated to my wife, Belinda, who has stood by me in times of lack and in times of abundance. I thank her for being a friend, a loving, supportive companion, and an excellent mother to our son, Robert Ephraim. I thank my daughters, Keisha and LaTeisha, both beautiful, talented, and loving young ladies. I also thank my wonderful parents, Albert and Luberta Bolden, who had been married fifty-two years before my Dad's passing in December 1999. I praise God for their support in all my endeavors. I thank my brother, Freddy L. Bolden, who led me to the Lord and has always been available when I needed him. I am also very grateful to my mother-in-law, Christine Keith, for her prayers and her willingness to assist wherever she could.

To my family: I love you all, and thanks for being a vital part of my life.

— Robert E. Bolden

TABLE OF CONTENTS

ACKNOWLEDGMENTS

I would be remiss if I did not acknowledge my pastor, Dr. Frederick K.C. Price, for teaching me the Word of God, and for demonstrating that he is a living example of what he teaches. I am grateful for having had the privilege of attending the Ministry Training Institute, a wonderful school for future ministers, which he established on the grounds of the world's greatest ministry, Crenshaw Christian Center. The revelation and information that I received from Dr. Price and other instructors have made tremendous deposits into my life, and I am now able to share them with others.

Both Dr. Price and his beautiful wife, Dr. Betty, will never know how honored I have been to play an active and involved part at CCC.

INTRODUCTION

Our heavenly Father desires that His children experience victory, prosperity, and good success in every area of life. In order to achieve these desires, it is important that we as Christians recognize that there are hostile spirits around us whose mission it is to derail God's plans to bless us. In other words, their main objective is to stop the believer from receiving financial prosperity.

There are millions of Christians all over the world who are doing all that they know to do to make it in life, yet they are bound by financial problems. They consistently study the Word; they make the right confessions; they pray in tongues, yet they are still struggling to keep their heads above the waters of lack and debt. It is true that there are many things that we as Christians must do in order to receive all the blessings that are promised us in God's Word. However, what every Christian needs to understand is that we face tremendous spiritual opposition. Demonic forces have been assigned to thwart the financial success of the children of God.

This book's purpose is to help you identify those robbing spirits and recognize their activity so that you can avert the attacks on your goods and command those spirits to return all that has been stolen from you and yours. The aim of Satan and his demon hordes is to stop the work of God in the earth. They will use any means available to accomplish this, including the bringing of sickness, disease, poverty, and a host of human ills. This book will focus on relieving one of those ills — the attack on your financial prosperity.

— Robert E. Bolden

1

CONFRONTATION WITH THE CANAANITES

God Almighty promised to deliver the children of Israel from Egyptian bondage and lead them into a land flowing with *milk* and *honey*. This was the good land that He led Abram to hundreds of years before, and promised to give him and his descendants as an inheritance — the land of Canaan. According to *The New Unger's Bible Dictionary*:

> *This graphic figure* [the term "flowing with milk and honey"] *portrays the fertile land supplying rich pasture for cattle, which give milk so abundantly that the land is said to flow with it, and producing many kinds of flowers, which provide food to honey-producing bees.*[1]

---

[1] Harrison, R.K., editor, *The New Unger's Bible Dictionary* (Chicago: Moody Press, 1988), 585.

The Hebrew word for *milk* is *chalab*, which means "richness." It indicates that the area had plenty of resources. The word *honey* is the Hebrew word *debash*, which means "to be gummy;" honey (from its stickiness) is a sweet, syrupy fluid. Honey is easily assimilated in the body. The two main sugars it contains — levulose and dextrose — are quickly converted into energy. The energy-giving properties of honey are illustrated in the case of Jonathan, the son of King Saul, who tasted honey when he was exhausted from battle, **and his eyes were enlightened** (1 Samuel 14:27).

Canaan was known for its prosperity. The term *Canaan* became synonymous with *merchant* or *trader*. But the spirit of Canaan inspires lust for material goods and operates through greed. The Canaanite spirit is behind all trade, finances, and the international economy of the world system. It is also a spirit of destruction and death, a spirit that attempts to draw Christians — like bees to honey — to an inordinate desire for material things and away from God. God wants His people to have the milk and honey, but He wants them to put Him first.

The spirit of materialism is seducing American society more than ever before. The Word of God shows us that this spirit is cursed and made to be servant of servants. In other words, the Canaanite spirit should serve us, the children of God. Genesis 9:25 says:

And he said, Cursed be Canaan; a servant of servants shall he be unto his brethren.

The derivation of the name *Canaan* is not clear. It probably comes from the Hebrew root word *kawnah* or *kana*, which means "to bend the knee; hence to humiliate, vanquish: — bring down (low), into subjection, under, humble (self), subdue."[2] Canaan was also known as "the land where the sun bows down, that is, sets in the evening, or the West Land."[3] *The New Smith Bible Dictionary* interprets "the land of Canaan" to mean "lowland," which likely applied to the coastland area inhabited by the Phoenicians.[4]

The term *Canaanite* became synonymous with the words *merchant* or *trader*, usually referring to the Phoenicians, who were involved in international commerce. While trading and merchandising were important to the growth of villages and towns, it brought its own peculiar problems, as the *HarperCollins Bible Dictionary* suggests:

> *Successful trade brought wealth (Ezekiel 28:5), but it could breed violence and corruption (Verse 16) leading to destruction (Verse 18). It was normal to invest resources (Luke 19:13), but traffic*

---

[2] James Strong, *Strong's Exhaustive Concordance of the Bible* (Grand Rapids, Michigan: Baker Book House, 1992), number 3667.

[3] *The Oxford Dictionary of the Jewish Religion*, (New York: Oxford University Press, 1997), 146.

[4] *The New Smith's Bible Dictionary* (New York: Doubleday & Company, 1966), 58.

in sacrifice materials was considered by Jesus to be an inappropriate use of the Jerusalem Temple precincts, as John's Gospel reports (John 2:16; see also Zechariah 14:21).[5]

In Ezekiel 28:5, the Lord is speaking directly to Satan, who apparently took control of trade and commerce early on. He says:

By thy great wisdom and by thy traffick [trade or merchandise] **hast thou increased thy riches, and thine heart is lifted up because of thy riches.**

Verses 16 and 18 say:

By the multitude of thy merchandise they have filled the midst of thee with violence, and thou has sinned: Therefore, I will cast thee as profane out of the mountain of God: and I will destroy thee, O covering cherub, from the midst of the stones of fire...

...Thou hast defiled thy sanctuaries by the multitude of thine iniquities, by the iniquity of thy traffick; therefore will I bring forth a fire from the midst of thee, it shall devour thee, and I will bring thee to ashes

---

[5] Paul J. Achtemeier, general editor, *HarperCollins Bible Dictionary*, (New York: HarperCollins Publishers, 1985), 1165.

upon the earth in the sight of all them that behold thee.

There is a strong suggestion in these scriptures of an unholy alliance between trade and corruption of the body and the spirit.

The word *Canaanite* refers to the race of people descending from Ham's son, Canaan, and to the land where they resided along the eastern Mediterranean between Egypt and Syria (Genesis 9:18; 10:6). "They [the Canaanites] include several peoples or tribes, but always numbered among them were the Canaanites proper, the Hittites, the Amorites, the Perizzites, the Jebusites, and the Hivites."[6]

The Amorites lived in the highlands; the Hittites settled in the hill country around Judah; the Jebusites in the area that became Jerusalem; the Perizzites in the low, unwalled towns in Ephraim, and the Hivites in tent settlements near Tyre. The country, later called Palestine, lay between the Mediterranean Sea and the mountains of Arabia.

God prepared the children of Israel to possess the Promised Land (or Canaan), that prosperous region inhabited by the "ites" — the Amorites, the Hittites, the Hivites, the Jebusites, and the Perizzites. The children of Israel knew of the Canaanites' debased character and the spirits that governed them. They knew that the "ites" were a cursed, demonically

---

[6] *The Oxford Dictionary,* 147.

controlled people with whom they were to have no association. They were warned that intermingling with the "ites" could cause Israel to be dispossessed of its rightful inheritance. According to *The New Unger's Bible Dictionary*:

> *Canaanite fertility cults are seen to be more base than elsewhere in the ancient world. The virile monotheistic faith of the Hebrews was continually in peril of contamination from the lewd nature worship with immoral gods, prostitute goddesses, serpents, cultic doves, and bulls.* [7]

God used Moses to bring the Hebrews out of Egypt after four hundred years of persecution in the land of the Pharaohs.

Exodus 3:7-8:

And the Lord said, I have surely seen the affliction of my people which are in Egypt, and have heard their cry by reason of their taskmasters; for I know their sorrows;

And I am come down to deliver them out of the hand of the Egyptians, and to bring them up out of that land unto a good land and large, unto a land flowing with milk and honey; unto the place of the Canaanites, and the Hittites, and the Amorites, the

---

[7] Unger, 202-203.

Perizzites, and the Hivites, and the Jebusites.

According to Exodus 34:10-11, the Lord made a covenant before all the people and did things that were never seen or done in all the earth. The Lord told Israel that He would drive out their enemies before them. That included the Amorites, the Canaanites, the Hittites, the Perizzites, the Hivites, and the Jebusites. He also warned Israel against making covenants with the "ites."

In Numbers 13:1 the Lord spoke to Moses and told him to send men to search the land of Canaan. When the men returned, they reported that the land was truly plentiful, flowing with milk and honey, but that the people — the "ites" — were strong that dwelled in the land. The Amorites dwelled in the mountains, and the Canaanites dwelled by the sea (Numbers 13:29).

The Bible says these spies brought back "an evil report"; that is, a report contrary to God's Word. In other words, they denied that they were able to possess the land that God had given them, because of the "ites" in the land. The spies focused on how gigantic the sons of Anak were in comparison to how small they themselves were. The spies complained that they were like grasshoppers in their own sight as well as in the giants' sight.

Those who believed the evil report perished in the wilderness and never saw the Promised Land. As

7

former slaves, they never arrived at the place of true freedom and biblical prosperity that God intended for them to have. Ten spies gave reports based upon what they saw, but two others — namely, Joshua and Caleb — gave reports based upon what God had said. Joshua and Caleb were the only adults who had been delivered from Egyptian bondage who were also permitted to enter the Promised Land. All other adults, from twenty years old and upward, died in the wilderness. Joshua and Caleb would live to finally accomplish God's great plan — at least some of it — of routing the Canaanites, Amorites, Jebusites, Hivites, Hittites and Perizzites from the land.

Israel's experience indicates that whenever God's people are about to enter into their inheritance, they will face spiritual opposition. The fact that there are giants in the land simply means that using His Word to overcome them provides greater opportunities to prove that God is faithful and true.

The Lord admonished the children of Israel to obey all His commandments so that they could possess the land that He swore to their fathers to give them. As we see in Deuteronomy 8:18, He said:

But thou shalt remember the Lord thy God: for it is he that giveth thee power to get wealth, that he may establish his covenant which he sware unto thy fathers, as it is this day.

When Moses died, Joshua led the children of Israel across the Jordan River into Canaan. It was

8

there, at the battle of Jericho, a walled city in Canaan, that Joshua demonstrated his God-given strategic skills, as he commanded the children of Israel to march around the city. The Book of Joshua shows how God's people answered the challenge to be free as they followed Him. Through Joshua, God brought them to deliverance.

Joshua 9:1-2:

And it came to pass, when all the kings which were on this side Jordan, in the hills, and in the valleys, and in all the coast of the great sea over against Lebanon, the Hittite, and the Amorite, the Canaanite, the Perizzite, the Hivite, and the Jebusite, heard thereof;

That they gathered themselves together, to fight with Joshua and with Israel, with one accord.

Although the people of Canaan were not united, the Bible says they joined together to fight Joshua and Israel. Clearly, Israel would not enter into its inheritance without a struggle, but the battle was the Lord's.

God constantly warned the children of Israel to drive out and destroy the Amorites, the Hittites, the Hivites, the Jebusites and the Perizzites. (There were several other "ites" that inhabited the land of Canaan, but the five listed here have certain characteristics

9

related to activities in the financial realm.) The spirits behind these "ites" can be called rulers of darkness, as indicated in Ephesians 6:12:

> **For we wrestle not against flesh and blood, but against principalities, against powers, against the rulers of the darkness of this world, against spiritual wickedness in high places.**

In the Greek language in which the New Testament was written, the word *darkness* in this context is the word *skotos,* which means "to restrain, to stop, or hinder."[8] The main objective of the "ites" is to delay, stop, or hinder finances. And they did this with deceptive tactics, usually in secrecy or under the cover of darkness.

Joshua informed the children of Israel that they had to be strong because they would face trials and tribulation before they received the land of Canaan as an inheritance. While Joshua was alive, they succeeded admirably in driving out the Canaanites. But after Joshua's death, they became disorganized. A new generation arose up that did not know the God who had delivered them from Egyptian bondage.

With Joshua gone, the people repeatedly fell into idolatry, came under political domination,

---

[8] *Strong's,* number 4655.

intermarried with the Canaanites, and committed grave abominations. These were the exact things about which God had warned them.

Judges 2:11-12:

And the children of Israel did evil in the sight of the Lord, and served Baalim:

And they forsook the Lord God of their fathers, which brought them out of the land of Egypt, and followed other gods, of the gods of the people that were round about them, and bowed themselves unto them, and provoked the Lord to anger.

Judges 3:5-6:

And the children of Israel dwelt among the Canaanites, Hittites, and Amorites, and Perizzites, and Hivites, and Jebusites:

And they took their daughters to be their wives, and gave their daughters to their sons, and served their gods.

Disobeying the Lord is very costly. When God delivered Israel out of Egypt, their God-given goal was to possess the Promised Land without becoming involved with the inhabitants while possessing it. As they began to disobey God and assimilate the Canaanite cultic practices, certain characteristics prevalent among the "ites" began to show up in Israel as well.

We need to recognize these so-called "ites" and understand their methods of operation. These are spirits committed to robbing believers of all that they have.

2

CHARACTERISTICS OF
THE CANAANITES

In studying the characteristics of the "ites" — the Amorites, the Hittites, the Hivites, the Jebusites and the Perizzites — we can understand why the Lord commanded Israel to destroy them. He wanted to prevent these spirits from working their lustful and destructive influence on Israel's social and economic systems. When the children of Israel failed to drive out the "ites," God confronted them in their disobedience, saying:

Judges 2:2-3:

... ye have not obeyed my voice: why have ye done this?

Wherefore I also said, I will not drive them out from before you; but they shall be as thorns in your sides, and their gods shall be a snare unto you.

Judges 3:5-6:

And the children of Israel dwelt among the Canaanites, Hittites, and Amorites, and Perizzites, and Hivites, and Jebusites:

And they took their daughters to be their wives, and gave their daughters to their sons, and served their gods.

One obvious example of the depravity of Canaan's line can be seen in Canaan's first son, Sidon, and his descendants. Sidon established a principal city in ancient Phoenicia, which he named for himself. The Sidonians were famous for craftsmanship in weaving and in their ability as loggers and lumbermen (1 Kings 5:6), but they practiced sexual orgies as a part of their worship of the goddess Ashtoreth, or Asherah.

This same influence is being exerted on economic systems today. It operates heavily behind the merchandising of goods and services. As an example, many advertisers employ some form of sexual come-ons and subliminal signals to sell their products, and these messages constantly challenge our traditional moral standards and family values.

We will examine how these spirits function, and how they attempt to bring destruction and poverty to the body of Christ.

1. AMORITE SPIRIT

This is the spirit of slander. *Amorite* comes from a root word that means "babbler, bitter, rebel and talkative."[9] The Amorite spirit sows thoughts of discord and division. It uses one to speak against another. This spirit uses condemnation to paralyze Christians, but God says in Amos 2:9-10:

> **Yet destroyed I the Amorite before them, whose height was like the height of the cedars, and he was strong as the oaks; yet I destroyed his fruit from above, and his roots from beneath.**

> **Also I brought you up from the land of Egypt, and led you forty years through the wilderness, to possess the land of the Amorite.**

Numbers 14:36 says:

> **And the men, which Moses sent to search the land, who returned, and made all the congregation to murmur against him, by bringing up a slander upon the land.**

Obviously, these men that Moses sent out had come in contact with the spirit of the Amorites, which is the spirit of slander. Numbers 13:29 says:

---

[9] *Strong's*, numbers 567, 559.

The Amalekites dwell in the land of the south; and the Hittites, and the Jebusites, and the Amorites, dwell in the mountains; and the Canaanites dwell by the sea, and by the coast of Jordan.

Titus 1:10 tells us:

For there are many unruly and vain talkers and deceivers, specially they of the circumcision.

This spirit can operate strongly through co-workers, acquaintances or even those who you may think are your friends — like Judas, who betrayed Jesus with a kiss. The Hebrew word for *confederate* is slander, babbler[10]; such persons can inflict deep wounds and damage another's character and reputation. The word *babbler* in Hebrew means "a master of the tongue."[11]

2. HITTITE SPIRIT

This is a spirit of fear, manifesting itself in those who are broken, or fearful. It instills doubt and unbelief. This spirit operates in churches and is mostly noted in the area of tithes and offerings. This spirit represented itself in the Hittites' aggressiveness in commerce. According to *The New Unger's Bible Dictionary*:

---

[10] *Strong's*, number 1167.
[11] *Unger's*, 133.

Many scholars consider the Hittites to be the third most influential of ancient peoples of the Middle East, rivaling the Egyptians and the Mesopotamians. Hebrews dreaded them as well as the empires on the Tigris and Euphrates.... Their aggressiveness is demonstrated also in their commercial activities.... [12]

The Hittite spirit affects Christians by making them fearful of giving and of handling financial matters. In the kingdom of God, however, if there is no giving there can be no receiving. The answer to defeating this fear is to give even more aggressively.

The Hittites were the sons of Heth, and Heth was the second son of Canaan. The name *Heth* means "terror."[13] It comes from the Canaanite word *chathath*, which means "to prostrate; hence to break down, either by violence or confusion and fear: — Abolish, affright, be (make) afraid, amaze, beat down, discourage, (cause to) dismay, go down, scare, terrify."[14]

Abraham, however, the friend of God, had no fear of the Hittites. When Sarah, his wife, died in Kirjath-abar, which was Hebron, the home of the Hittites, he communed with them before purchasing a burial place for her (Genesis 23:8). Abraham and

---

[12] *Unger's,* 580.
[13] Strong's, number 2845.
[14] Strong's, number 2865.

the Hittites were extremely polite and respectful to one another. Clearly, the fearsome Hittites were more fearful of Abraham because they knew he was a friend of God whose reputation had preceded him.

Genesis 23:5-16:

And the children of Heth answered Abraham, saying unto him,

Hear us, my lord: thou art a mighty prince [prince of God] among us: in the choice of our sepulchers bury thy dead; none of us shall withhold from thee his sepulcher, but that thou mayest bury thy dead.

And Abraham stood up, and bowed himself to the people of the land, even to the children of Heth.

And he communed with them, saying, If it be your mind that I should bury my dead out of my sight; hear me, and entreat for me Ephron the son of Zohar.

That he may give me the cave of Machpe'- lah, which he hath, which is in the end of his field; for as much money as it is worth he shall give it me for a possession of a burying place amongst you.

And Ephron dwelt among the children of Heth: and Ephron the Hittite answered Abraham in the audience of the children of

Heth, even of all that went in at the gate of his city, saying,

Nay, my lord, hear me: the field give I thee, and the cave that is therein, I give it thee: bury thy dead.

And Abraham bowed down himself before the people of the land.

And he spake unto Ephron in the audience of the people of the land, saying, But if thou wilt give it, I pray thee, hear me: I will give thee money for the field: take it of me, and I will bury my dead there.

And Ephron answered Abraham, saying unto him,

My lord, hearken unto me: the land is worth four hundred shek'-els of silver: what is that betwixt me and thee: bury therefore thy dead.

And Abraham hearkened unto Ephron; and Abraham weighed to Ephron the silver, which he had named in the audience of the sons of Heth, four hundred shek'-els of silver, current money with the merchant.

These aggressive merchants were like putty in Abraham's hand. Indeed, Ephron would have given Abraham the land if he had accepted it. But Abraham was not the type to let a heathen enrich him, a prince of God. Here is one other insight: Two of the meanings of the word *communed*[15] are "to subdue" and "to destroy." If nothing else, Abraham subdued these Hittites.

3. HIVITE SPIRIT

The Hivite spirit is a spirit of deception. The word *Hivite* means "villager and wickedness." As a villager (business partner) this spirit works through others by disguising themselves as someone with ordinary good motives. It is a spirit of seduction, causing the simple to part with their money through get-rich-quick schemes and wrong deals. On the surface, this spirit may appear as powerful, but just as Laban deceived Jacob in Genesis 29:16-25 and 31:7, it can deceive Christians and other people today.

Let's look at a classic example of how this spirit manifests itself:

Gibeon, Chephirah, Beeroth, and Kirjath-jearim were Hivite cities that, through deception, were able to enter into a treaty with Joshua and the children of Israel. When the Gibeonites heard how Joshua destroyed Jericho and Ai, they devised a plan to save themselves.

Joshua 9:1-6 says:

And it came to pass, when all the kings which were on this side Jordan, in the hills,

---

[15] Strong's, number 1696.

and in the valleys, and in all the coasts of the great sea over against Lebanon, the Hittite, and the Amorite, the Canaanite, the Perizzite, the Hivite, and the Jebusite, heard thereof;

That they gathered themselves together, to fight with Joshua and with Israel, with one accord.

And when the inhabitants of Gibeon heard what Joshua had done unto Jericho and to Ai,

They did work wilily, and went and made as if they had been ambassadors, and took old sacks upon their asses, and wine bottles, old, and rent, and bound up;

And old shoes and clouted upon their feet, and old garments upon them; and all the bread of their provision was dry and mouldy.

And they went to Joshua unto the camp at Gilgal, and said unto him, and to the men of Israel. We be come from a far country: now therefore make ye a league with us.

In fact, the Gibeonites lived nearby and were among the people God had warned Israel to destroy. Because of the way they looked and the condition of their clothes and food, the men of Israel were taken in by the deception because ... **they asked not counsel at the mouth of the Lord** (Joshua 9:14).

21

Joshua 9:15:

And Joshua made peace with them, and made a league with them, to let them live: and the princes of the congregation sware unto them.

But in Joshua 9:22-23, when Joshua found out about the deception, he

. . . called for them, and he spake unto them, saying, Wherefore have ye beguiled us, saying, We are very far from you; when you dwell among us?

Now therefore ye are cursed, and there shall none of you be freed from being bondmen, and hewers of wood and drawers of water from the house of my God.

So Israel had a partner that they did not seek or want, and immediately the Gibeonites became a burden to them. When the Amorite kings heard what Gibeonites — who were supposed to be in league with the Amorites and other Canaanites — had done, they made war on the Gibeonites. Joshua and Israel, therefore, were forced to defend the Gibeonites because they had made a treaty with them. By this we can see how important it is to seek God before entering into such binding relationships, whether in business or politics. Such spirits can cause Christians to waste time and money, sometimes ending in court cases trying to defend their rights or person against someone with whom they never should have been involved in the first place.

2 Corinthians 6:14:

Be not unequally yoked together with unbelievers: for what fellowship hath righteousness with unrighteousness: and what communion hath light with darkness?

4. JEBUSITE SPIRIT

This is the spirit of heaviness. *Jebusite* means to "tread underfoot, or trample down." This spirit attacks the emotions with negativity. It saps confidence and strength. Its main objective is to instigate the feeling of resignation, to give up or quit. This spirit will attempt to make believers lose their vision, purpose, and dreams. This is why believers must write their vision down and keep it before their eyes daily. Jebus, whose name means "trodden place," was the third son of Canaan. Jebus was probably the original name of Jerusalem, whose citadel contained the impregnable stronghold of Zion. We can see in 2 Samuel 5:6-7 how the Jebusites tried to frustrate and discourage David in battle:

And the king and his men went to Jerusalem unto the Jebusites, the inhabitants of the land: which spake unto David, saying, Except thy take away the blind and the lame, thou shalt not come in hither: thinking, David cannot come in hither.

Nevertheless David took the strong hold of Zion: the same is the city of David.

This Jebusite spirit is more than likely what influenced ten of the twelve spies to return with an evil report, saying that Israel could not take the land. Numbers 13:27-29 says:

And they told him [Moses], and said, We came unto the land whither thou sentest us, and surely it floweth with milk and honey; and this is the fruit of it.

Nevertheless the people be strong that dwell in the land, and the cities are walled, and very great; and moreover we saw the children of Anak there.

The Amalekites dwell in the land of the south; and the Hittites, and the Jebusites, and the Amorites, dwell in the mountains; and the Canaanites dwell by the sea, and by the coast of Jordan.

What a sorry pack of spies this group made! They had seen the Promised Land and proven that it flowed with milk and honey, but they didn't believe that the God who led them through the Red Sea on dry land could also lead them into this land victoriously.

5. PERIZZITE SPIRIT

This is a robbing spirit. The word *Perizzite* means "to dispose of or dwell in unwalled city." The aim of this spirit is to steal and dispose of all you have built. The tribe of Judah (praise) destroyed the Perizzites (Judges 1:4). Through this spirit you will see characteristics of unfaithfulness and disloyalty, not honoring agreements.

Ezekiel 38:11-12:

And thou shalt say, I will go up to the land of unwalled villages; I will go to them that are at rest that dwell safely, all of them dwelling without walls, and having neither bars nor gates,

To take a spoil, and to take a prey; to turn thine hand upon the desolate places that are now inhabited, and upon the people that are gathered out of the nations, which have gotten cattle and goods that dwell in the midst of the land.

Even today, archaeologists are unsure of where the Perizzites originated. Far less is known about them than the other major Canaanite groups. These are people who detested walls, or any restriction against their coming and going. The lack of walls made their entrance and exit easy, but it also left the cities open to plunder by marauding invaders. Remember how Nehemiah struggled to restore the walls around Jerusalem? Whether he was aware of the Perizzite influence it is hard to say, but he knew the city could not be protected without walls.

This Perizzite spirit manifests itself where believers do not take proper precautions to preserve themselves and the things with which they have been entrusted. Christians who do not maintain savings accounts, make sound investments, or carry proper insurance — life, health, car, homeowners, burial, and business insurance, just to name a few — are affected by this spirit. A lapse in any one of these areas can destroy an individual or family financially.

Also, those who fail to tithe or give offerings are setting themselves up to be taken over by these robbing forces. These are God-robbers, and they live under a curse.

Malachi 3:8-12 says:

Will a man rob God? Yet ye have robbed me. But ye say, Wherein have we robbed thee? In tithes and offerings.

Ye are cursed with a curse: for ye have robbed me, even this whole nation.

Bring ye all the tithes into the storehouse, that there may be meat in mine house, and prove me now herewith, saith the Lord of hosts, if I will not open you the windows of heaven, and pour you out a blessing, that there shall not be room enough to receive it.

And I will rebuke the devourer for your sakes, and he shall not destroy the fruits of your ground; neither shall your vine cast

her fruit before the time in the field, saith the Lord of hosts.

And all nations shall call you blessed: for ye shall be a delightsome land, saith the Lord of hosts.

3

THE TRUE OWNER OF ALL WEALTH

The world's system is controlled by a high-ranking prince named Mammon (Matthew 6:24). The word *mammon* comes from the Aramaic word for riches or wealth. Mammon manifests itself in many forms throughout the world as the "creator of prosperity," but we know from the Word of God that that is not true. Jehovah God owns everything. He is *El Elyon*, creator and possessor of heaven and earth.

There are numerous Bible references that support God's ownership of the earth, including Psalm 24:1, which tells us that **the earth is the Lord's and the fullness thereof; the world and they that dwell therein.** In Psalm 50:10, God declares, **For every beast of the forest is mine, and the cattle upon a thousand hills.** Verse 12 says, **...for the world is mine, and the**

fullness thereof. A further reference of God's ownership is Haggai 2:8, where the Lord of host says, **the silver is mine, and the gold is mine.**

Poverty on the earth is a direct result of manipulation and control by the spirit of mammon. The name *mammon*[16] is Greek for *Mammonas*, which means "wealth personified." It also means "merchant" or "trader." Sound familiar? We have already found that the term *Canaanite* also means "merchant" or "trader." Mammon inspires lust for material gain — or greed. Another word that is synonymous with mammon is *avarice*, which means "greed," or "to have an excessive or insatiable desire for wealth or gain."

The spirit of mammon exerts its most powerful influence through strongholds. Strongholds are systems of thinking that are contrary to the Word of God. But the Word tells us in 2 Corinthians 10:4 that **the weapons of our warfare are not carnal, but mighty through God to the pulling down of strong holds.**

In Proverbs 13:22, the Bible says the wealth of the sinner is laid up for the just, and we as children of God are the just. The word *wealth* is the Hebrew word *chayil*,[17] which means "might, strength, power, army, forces, as well as riches." The Word of God also declares, **But thou shalt remember the Lord thy God: for it is he that giveth thee power to get wealth, that he**

---

[16] *Strong's*, number 3126.
[17] *Strong's*, number 2428.

29

may establish his covenant which he sware unto thy fathers, as it is this day (Deuteronomy 8:18).

The wealth being spoken of in this reference is enormous. A recent study by *Fortune 500* magazine concluded that if the wealth of the United States were divided equally among its citizens, each person would receive approximately $12 million dollars.[18]

But the article also stated that within a very short time, that money would find its way back into the hands of those who held it before, clearly implying that most people do not have the wisdom to manage such large sums of money. In other words, most people would quickly squander their fortunes through bad investments and unwise purchases — or be swindled out of them. What the article did not take into account is that there are spiritual forces that are constantly at work helping a few hoarders amass great fortunes and keeping the money out of the hands of most people, especially the believers.

The spirit realm affects us more than most Christians realize, and no one takes more delight in the church's ignorance than the powers of darkness. Most Christians don't understand that we as believers are engaged in spiritual warfare, and riches are necessary to keep the enemy at bay.

---

[18] *Wealth Management for the Sophisticated Investor*, Fortune 500, April 2000.

Ephesians 6:12:

For we wrestle not against flesh and blood, but against principalities, against powers, against the rulers of the darkness of this world, against spiritual wickedness in high places.

In John 10:10, Jesus tells us that **the thief cometh not, but for to steal, and to kill, and to destroy**. When these spirits attack our finances, we must counterattack with God's Word.

That Word of God tells us in Proverbs 6:30-31 that there is a thief, and if you find him he must restore sevenfold. This means he must return to us seven times the amount he stole. Clearly, the amount of money stolen from Christians is enormous, and we have been given the ability to identify the thief and claim what belongs to us.

"There is more personal wealth in America today than ever before — in excess 23 trillion dollars. Several factors account for this. The bull market, widespread usage of stock options, and record-breaking levels of entrepreneurship are among them," continued the *Fortune 500* article.[19] The article also said that "the market is more and more comprised of wealth creators versus wealth inheritors." The number of wealthy Americans is growing at an

---

[19] Fortune 500.

unprecedented pace. As of July 1999, there were 17 million households with a net worth in excess of $500,000. But by 2020, that number will hit 20 million, Walter H. Zultowski, senior vice president for marketing and market research at Phoenix Home Life Mutual Insurance Company, told Fortune 500.

We are in a wonderful time in the body of Christ, and we must ask God for wisdom to handle the wealth that is coming into the kingdom. We are the generation that has the revelation on how this wealth will end up in our hands. The Word of God clearly shows us that it is the will of God for the New Testament church to see this wealth transferred from the sinner into the Church's hands.

Isaiah 45:2-3:

I will go before thee, and make the crooked places straight: I will break in pieces the gates of brass, and cut in sunder the bars of iron:

And I will give thee the treasures of darkness, and hidden riches of secret places, that thou mayest know that I, the Lord, which call thee by my name, am the God of Israel.

Isaiah 61:6 says something equally interesting:

But ye shall be named the Priest of the Lord: men shall call you the Ministers of our God: ye shall eat the riches of the

Gentiles, and in their glory shall ye boast yourselves.

Job 27:16-17 give us further confirmation:

Though he heap up silver as the dust, and prepare raiment as the clay;

He may prepare it, but the just shall put it on, and the innocent shall divide the silver.

Clearly, these verses point to a time when a great transfer of wealth will occur. Those who get in on it will more than likely be those who are tithers. All others reside under a curse.

4

STRATEGIES FOR RECOVERING STOLEN GOODS

N ow that we've established that the earth's wealth is stored up for God's children, here are three strategies to help you recover those stolen goods:

1. IDENTIFY THE THIEF

The Bible clearly states in John 10:10 that the thief cometh — he *will* show up! As part of our weaponry, God has given us certain spiritual gifts. First Corinthians 12:10 talks about the gift of discerning of spirits, which means that God can, and will, give us the ability to know when and where evil spirits are in operation. Verse 31 says to covet earnestly the best gifts. Our heavenly Father says to ask and *we will receive* when we pray and ask in faith. He will show us which spirit is attempting to attack our finances. Faith is the key to receiving.

The Word of God states that if you find the thief, he is to restore sevenfold and shall give all the substance of his house (Proverbs 6:31). The reason for restoring seven times the owed amount is because seven is the number of completion. Therefore, the devil must completely cooperate and give back all that he has stolen.

2. ATTACK THE SPIRIT

After you have identified which spirit has attacked your finances or circumstances, you must counterattack in the name of Jesus. We must attack it violently with warfare prayers, or verbal commands using the name of Jesus. We must also bind them and render them powerless and restrain their attacks (Matthew 18:18). Many Christians may not understand what I mean when I speak of *warfare prayers*. These are prayers where you use the name of Jesus to speak to a situation, condition, atmosphere, thing, or spirit. Jesus says in Mark 11:24, **"Therefore I say unto you, what things soever ye desire, when ye pray, believe that ye received them and ye shall have them."**

Whatever you desire that is consistent with the Word of God and with faith in the name of Jesus will be manifested in your life. When we attack the powers of darkness and any demonic activity by using the Word of God, we are putting a stop to their main

function, which is to steal, to kill, and to destroy. And
we must understand that delays to answered prayers
are not necessarily denials from God. We know this
from Daniel 10:12-13. Daniel prayed and his prayer
was heard the moment he prayed, but his answer was
delayed by the prince of Persia, an evil spirit that
operated behind the ruler of that nation. The angel
Michael was sent with the answer, but he was hindered
by the evil spirit who was in control of the country.

In Exodus 33:2, the Bible shows us that God will
indeed send an angel to war on our behalf. The Bible
also tells us that the angels have been sent to minister for us who are heirs of salvation (Hebrews 1:14).
The Greek word for *salvation* is *soteria*, which means
"rescue, safety, deliverance, and health." In this case,
it means being rescued from poverty, lack, and all
demonic activity that attempts to hinder finances from
reaching us.

3. DEMAND FULL RESTORATION

This is a step that is most important but often
overlooked in receiving what was stolen: Demand full
restoration! The Word of God clearly states that if the
thief is caught, he must restore sevenfold. The Hebrew word for *restore* is *shalom*. This is one of the most
pregnant words in the Hebrew language, commonly
translated as "peace" or "prosperity." In Proverbs
6:30-31, the Word says:

**Men do not despise a thief, if he steals to
satisfy his soul when he is hungry; but if**

he be found, he shall restore sevenfold; he shall give all the substance of his house.

In the context of this scripture, the word *restore* means "to repay in full restitution or to amend." We have every legal right to strip all wealth under control of these spirits — Amorite, Hittite, Hivite, Jebusite or Perizzite — especially when they attack our finances.

In Joel 2:25, the Word tells us that the Lord will restore or replace the years the locust, the cankerworm, the caterpillars, and the palmerworm have eaten. These are types of demonic forces that take from the people of God and destroy their wealth. The word *locust* means "rapid increase,"[20] *cankerworm* means "to lick up and devour,"[21] *caterpillar* means "to consume as a ravager,"[22] and *palmerworm* means "a kind of locust that devours."[23]

However, double restoration comes when we pray for our friends. The Hebrew word *friend* is *ray-ah*, which means "an associate." The reason it is important to know the meaning of the word *friend* here is because of the distinction between a true friend and an associate. Associates are those with whom we work or otherwise have dealings, but who may not mean

---

[20] *Strong's*, number 7235.
[21] *Strong's*, number 3218.
[22] *Strong's*, number 2625.
[23] *Strong's*, number 1501.

us well. The Hebrew word *raw-ah*, which means to "tend to like a flock, keep company with, companion," denotes a true friend.

In the Book of Job, we see Job depicted as a man of high moral character. Even after a series of misfortunes and deep sufferings, he remained faithful to God. The Lord "turned the captivity" of Job when Job prayed for his friends. Also, the Lord gave Job twice as much as he had before (Job 42:10). After we have done what the Word of God says, we should praise and worship God in faith for the manifestation. When the manifestation comes and God prospers us, we must realize that it is not all for show, but to *sow*!

As New Testament believers, we know that Jesus our Lord, Savior, and coming King, has totally defeated every principality and power, including Satan. He has "spoiled principalities and powers" and made a show of them openly, triumphing over them (Colossians 2:15). Jesus has given us His power to be successful in every aspect of life.

Luke 10:19:

Behold, I give unto you, power to tread [walk on] serpents and scorpions, and over all the power of the enemy.

The Greek word *power* in this context is translated *exousia*, which means "authority, and jurisdiction" over serpents and scorpions. The word *serpent* is synonymous with Satan and demons. It is the Greek word *ophis*, which means sharpness of vision. A snake, particularly a viper, is an artful, sly, cunning, malicious creature that usually sees you well before you see it.

We must be ever mindful that while we are busy doing the work of the Lord, people are watching us, and will allow the enemy to use them through jealousy or envy to hinder us from achieving our goals. But we have the ability, authority, and jurisdiction over serpents and scorpions.

5

USING YOUR POWER AND AUTHORITY

As we apply the Word of God to every situation in our lives, especially in the area of finances, we are assured that the Word will do what God said it would do. Our responsibility is to apply the Word and believe it. As Joshua did to the five Amorite kings in Joshua 10:15-27, when he trapped them in a cave and ultimately hanged them, we must do to these five controlling spirits that are presently in our Promised Land. They may appear to be giants, but they are easily defeated, just as David defeated Goliath.

The following is a summary and a quick reference guide to the spirits that can hinder your progress and prosperity:

AMORITE — Slander, talkative, sows thoughts of discord. (Proverbs. 6:19; 10:18; 18:8; Ephesians 4:29)

HITTITE — Fear, doubt, and unbelief. (Matthew 21:21-22; Mark 9:24; 2 Timothy 1:7)

HIVITE — Deception, villager, wickedness. Get-rich-quick schemes and wrong deals. (Mark 13:5-6; Galatians 6:7; 2 Timothy. 3:13)

JEBUSITE — Heaviness. Attacks the emotions, saps confidence and strength. (Proverbs 12:25; Matthew 11:28-30)

PERIZZITE — Robber. Steals and attempts to dispose of what has been built. (Proverbs 6:30-31; Joel 2:25; John 10:10)

Isaiah 1:19 says, **if you are willing and obedient you shall eat the good of the land.** The Book of Job declares that those who obey and serve Him shall spend their days in prosperity and their years in pleasures. When we are obedient to the Word of God and operate in faith, our heavenly Father clearly reveals to us through the Word what our inheritance means and encompasses. Remember, He said in Isaiah 45:2-3:

> **I will go before thee, and make the crooked places straight: I will break in pieces the gates of brass, and cut in sunder the bars of iron:**

> **And I will give thee the treasures of darkness and hidden riches of secret places, that thou mayest know that I, the Lord, which call thee by thy name, am the God of Israel.**

The Father says He will give us treasures of darkness. The Hebrew word for *treasure* is *owtsar,* meaning depository or armory, or a place to store up treasures.

The word *hidden* means a secret storehouse, "buried money." The words *secret places* mean a covert or covered place. In other words, God has great and valuable resources stored up for us.

There are places where money is buried that only God Almighty knows. The key is to desire to be a blessing to the people of God (Matthew 6:33), and know that the wealth of the wicked is laid up for the just (Proverbs 13:22).

There is also a very potent force released in prayer that moves the hand of God. When you desire to bless the body of Christ in the area of finances or material prosperity, then the powers of darkness work overtime to try to hinder you, but God is faithful.

I am committed to my assignment and responsibilities, conducting my affairs with the highest degree of integrity, dedicated to serving in the household of God by walking in love and consistently tithing and giving offerings. (Remember, you cannot prosper under the curse of a non-tither.)

6

PRAYER FOR FINANCES

If you're being continually harassed in your financial life, there's a good chance that one or more of these robbing spirits is the source of the problem. Here is a prayer that you can pray that will put an immediate halt to the attack — if you are praying in faith. It would be advisable to say this prayer daily, until you can repeat it by heart. By that time you will have developed a strong belief in these words.

Heavenly Father, in the name of Jesus, I thank You for revealing to me the names of the spirits that have attempted to hinder finances from reaching me and destroying my peace of mind.

Spirit of Mammon, according to Matthew 18:18, what I bind on earth shall be bound in heaven, and what I loose on earth shall be loosed in heaven. I bind your powers from operating against me to steal or block creative money-making thoughts from reaching me. I command you to loose every money-making thought you have stolen or blocked from me in Jesus' name. According to Proverbs 6:31, you have been found. According to Mark 3:27, once I have bound the strongman I can spoil his goods, so I take back every creative money-making idea that has been blocked or stolen from me in Jesus' name.

Amorite spirit, according to Proverbs 10:18, I bind your powers from operating against me to cause me to slander, to entice me to babble, rebel, be talkative, or bitter in Jesus' name. You will cease and desist from sowing thoughts of discord and division. You will not bring condemnation to paralyze me in Jesus' name. I am free from slander, babbling, talking, rebelling, bitterness, division, and discord in Jesus' name.

Hittite spirit, according to 2 Timothy 1:7 and Matthew 21:21-22, I bind your powers from operating against me to break me or to cause me to be fearful. The activities of doubt and unbelief are bound in Jesus' name. I command you to loose me from fear, doubt, and unbelief. Therefore, I am free in Jesus' name. For I have not been given the spirit of fear, but of power and love and of a sound mind.

Hivite spirit, according to Mark 13:5-6, I recognize you as a deceiver, and I take authority over you in the name of Jesus. You will not bring deception and wickedness to me. As a villager (a deceitful friend), you will no longer disguise yourself as someone ordinary. You will not seduce me to part with my money through get-rich-quick schemes and wrong deals. I command you to go in the name of Jesus, and I claim back every dollar I have spent or invested in schemes and wrong deals in Jesus' name.

Jebusite spirit, according to Matthew 11:28-30, I take authority over you. The spirit of heaviness will not operate against me. You will no longer tread me underfoot or attack my emotions with negativity. You will not attempt to sap my confidence and strength. I command you to cease and desist from instigating the feeling of resignation and the idea to give up or quit. Your powers are broken in the name of Jesus.

Perizzite spirit, according to John 10:10, **the thief cometh not, but for to steal, and to kill and to destroy**. Proverbs 6:31 says if I find the thief, he shall restore sevenfold. You have been found and you will no longer cause me to dwell in the unwalled city. You will no longer steal and dispose of what I have built in Jesus name. So, I take back everything you have stolen that I have built in Jesus' name.

Father, I thank You for Your Word. Isaiah 55:11 says, **So shall my word be that goeth forth out of my mouth: It shall not return unto me void, but it shall accomplish that which I please, and it shall prosper in the thing whereto I sent it.**

Exodus 33:2 says, **And I will send an angel before thee; and I will drive out the Canaanite, the Amorite, and the Hittite, the Perizzite, the Hivite, and the Jebusite**.

Hebrews 1:14 tells me that angels are all ministering spirits sent forth to minister for them who shall

45

be heirs of salvation. I have inherited salvation through what Jesus Christ did on the cross.

I thank You that Your Word declares in Joel 2:25, **And I will restore to you the years that the locust hath eaten, the cankerworm, and the caterpillar and the palmerworm....** I believe that I have received everything restored and replaced in Jesus' name. Ministering angels, I commission you to go forth to the north, the south, the east and the west to bring back the goods and cause them to manifest in answered prayer, in the name of Jesus.

Father, I thank You for revealing to me these truths in the areas of financial resources to help get the gospel out. Your Word also declares in Proverbs 13:22 that **a good man leaveth an inheritance to his children's children: and the wealth of the sinner is laid up for the just.**

And finally, Father, Matthew 11:12 says, **And from the days of John the Baptist until now the kingdom of heaven suffereth violence, and the violent take it by force.**

I thank You, Father, for this revelation about finances, and I am now violently against the powers of darkness. In Jesus' name, amen.